OUR HERI ı AGE: THE BIBLE

THE BIBLE
THE ELIMINATIONS FROM THE BIBLE
RESTATEMENTS OF THE BIBLE
THE BIBLE UNDER ATTACK
BIBLICAL FACTORS
THE BIBLE DIVINELY CONFIRMED

BY
REV. W. PASCOE GOARD

THE COVENANT PUBLISHING CO. LTD.
121, Low Etherley, Bishop Auckland, Co. Durham, DL14 0HA

2010

First Edition 1926
Reprinted 1941
Revised and reprinted 2010

ISBN 978-085205-072-9

Printed by
THE COVENANT PUBLISHING COMPANY LIMITED
121, Low Etherley, Bishop Auckland,
Co. Durham, DL14 0HA
www.covpub.co.uk

PREFACE

The modern reader will notice that there are some points and attitudes which appear very dated. Historical events since 1926 and developments in prophetic fulfilment and understanding would result in different interpretations if the book were to be written today. Nevertheless Rev. Pascoe Goard wrote very powerfully in support of the Bible and his words remain very helpful to those wishing to counter the objections and criticisms which are still raised.

THE PUBLISHERS

The following Obituary notice was sent to *The Times, Daily Telegraph* and *Morning Post.*

"On Wednesday morning, Dr. William Pascoe Goard, who was one of the leaders of the British-Israel Movement, passed peacefully away at the College, Harrow Weald. He was 74 years of age, and had completed 40 years ministry in the Methodist Church.

Born in Cornwall, he had lived for the greater part of his life in Canada.

He became a Vice-President of the British-Israel-World Federation in 1921, and was Editor of the weekly religious journal *The National Message.*

As a public speaker he attracted large audiences and as a writer his name was well known throughout all the British Dominions and the United States. In addition, he was Principal of the Garrison Bible College at Harrow Weald.

He was a man of outstanding ability whose loss will be widely felt throughout the whole English speaking world."

*   *   *   *   *

Dr. Goard was scheduled to speak at Denison House on Wednesday February 3rd at 3 and 7pm.

On February 6th a notice was posted in *The National Message*:

"Dr. Goard has been advised by his doctors that he should not undertake any lectures or platform speaking until they give their consent."

In the February 13th issue of *The National Message* a letter was printed, dated Monday 8th February:

"To the Editor, *The National Message.*

SIR – the world-wide sympathy with a devotion to Dr. W. Pascoe Goard, and his unique position in International circles of religious thought, call for some authoritative report upon his present condition of ill-health.

Fifteen years of strenuous exertion in administrative work and public education have taken their toll of a system always strained to capacity, but always deprived of adequate personal care and ease. We all know how he has invariably sacrificed himself on the altar of his ideal of Duty without thought for his personal comfort and convenience.

The last tour, involving 50,000 miles of continual travelling and lecturing under climatic conditions varying between the Arctic and the Torrid, and without due regard to the comforts demanded by his age, have proved too much for his physical frame. As a result of this, his flesh is failing though his will is still indomitable and the spirit fresh, forceful, steadfast and far-fixed as ever.

Humanly speaking, no effort – surgical or medical – has been, or will be, spared, and he is fighting as heartily in this cause as he has always fought for Right and Righteousness in the Great Cause. But his fighting days are done, and no official worries must be allowed to come his way until rest and care have somewhat restored his strength.

To the untiring, watchful care and skill of Mrs. Goard he and his medical friends owe more than can be said.

May Almighty God in His omniscient beneficence watch and ward over both.

I am, Sir, yours, etc.
B. WINTER GONIN, M.R.C.S. (ENG.), L.R.C.P. (LOND.)"

Editorial tribute to Dr. Goard by A.R.Heaver in *The National Message*, Saturday February 20th, 1937:

"KNOW YE NOT THAT THERE IS A GREAT MAN FALLEN THIS DAY IN ISRAEL?

With the passing of Dr. William Pascoe Goard, the British-Israel movement has lost a man of outstanding character and princely attainment. Truly a great man has fallen this day in Israel. It is difficult to pay just tribute to the memory of one who was the outstanding exponent of our teaching, and whose inspired labours lifted the presentation of our theme upon a new and higher plane of thought.

The words of *Corinthians* seem supremely appropriate when we think of him: ***"There is one glory of the sun, and another of the moon, and another glory of the stars: for one star differeth from another star in glory."*** His light was one of the first magnitude, and he let it shine before men with such unclouded brilliance that many were moved to glorify the name of the father in heaven.

Appropriate too are the words of the prophetic promise: ***"They that be wise shall shine as the brightness of the firmament; and they that turn many to righteousness as the stars for ever and ever."*** That is a Divine assurance for the Time of the End during which we live today. Our well-loved friend was a wise teacher – an unrivalled expositor of the sacred Scriptures – whose inspired writings illuminated many minds and led them to a knowledge of salvation through faith in the Son of God, the Father of lights. As a fervent evangelist his flaming words turned many thousands to righteousness, animating them with new resolve to live a more holy life.

Death cannot quench love. And we know that if a great man has fallen this day in Israel, it is only that he may be raised again in higher realms to an endless life of greater service.

So from the other side of the Veil his love will still inspire us, and his light will shine as the brightness of the firmament, as we enshrine the remembrance of his faithful witness in our hearts. So it will be until the perfect day when Christ, Who is our light, shall appear.

In honouring the memory of the one we loved it is incumbent upon us to rededicate our lives in unselfish service to Almighty God. That is the most fitting tribute we can pay to the one whose shining example was so much admired."

OUR HERITAGE

THE BIBLE

L et us look at the Bible as we possess it to-day, and ask: Is this book what we should have been led to expect it to be under all the circumstances, assuming it to be inspired of God; spoken by men so inspired?

Mark "Holy men of God spake as they were moved by the Holy Ghost." The word was spoken by men, inspired of God.

Assuming this fact, is the book such as we should expect it to be?

Let us pursue the question, What should we expect the Bible to be, assuming the fact that it was inspired of God; written by holy men of God?

We should expect it to be a handbook of life in all its phases. Purely human sciences study and seek to explain life in all its phases. The Bible must do no less.

It must deal with the body. Anatomy, Physiology, Pathology and so on must have a place in its writings.

It must deal with the mind in all its phases. Psychology in all its phases must have a place in the weaving of its pages.

It must deal with the spirit of man. In his Godward aspirations man must find an instructor and guide; and in his relationship with his neighbour, in every department of sociology, the Bible must mark the way.

The sciences have been enriched and confused by the libraries and literatures which have been produced by men not inspired of God. No man may hope in a long lifetime to read all the contributions of scientific men in all these departments.

The Bible enters every such field, not to explain and to teach, but to use every such department of activity rather for practical purposes than for the purpose of enquiry. The message of the Bible shows an understanding of every detail of the human frame. The message of the Bible shows a mastery of every fold of the human brain, and of every phase of the human mind. Its message is perfectly fitted to the mind addressed. The Bible shows more than human understanding of the things of the spirit. It puts the reader in the path which leads to God; and it gives him power to ascend into the Kingdom of God; it gives to him power to become the son of God.

Such a revelation must deal with nature. It must deal with the earth and with its origin and destiny. To make the mistake of wrongly dealing with the earth would be to manifest feet of clay, rather than to manifest Divine inspiration.

So, in the telling of the origin of the earth, the story must coincide with the record of the rocks as laid bare by geology. This test the Bible triumphantly sustains.

The Bible must be right in regard to astronomy. The earth must be part of the solar system. A severe test this, for who might suppose that primitive man or the men of the days of the beginnings of the Bible knew anything about the solar system. Yet the Bible tells of the place of the earth in the firmament of the solar system with unfaltering voice.

Even the most modern astronomical discoveries have a place within its pages. So we find the relativity of Einstein antedated in the first chapter of Genesis.

The Bible must be right in the realm of earthly life. Thus it tells the story of primordial vegetation, and of a period of animal life wherein "great whales" (monsters) existed on the planet earth.

Then the Bible proceeds to tell of the finer vegetable and the higher forms of animal life such as are found to-day.

The Bible gives to us an archaic creation including man. It then proceeds to give to us the history of the family of Adam and his seed. Thus in the realm of Botany, Zoology, Anthropology, the Bible stands the test.

The Bible must be true to history. From the formation of Adam and the birth of Seth (or appointed seed) down to the time of Our Lord the Bible tells a continuous and connected historical story elsewhere unparalleled. Like the lines of communication of an advancing army, the whole line of Biblical history is open to attack from every quarter, scientific and historic. Yet at every point where science or history has been able to bring to bear actual knowledge upon the story of the Bible, the Bible has been found to be correct in the main statements of its wonderful story. In the twelfth chapter of the Bible we are introduced to a city the very memory of which had passed away millenniums ago, Ur of the Chaldees. It has been reserved for the men of the twentieth century, and the present decade, to unearth that ancient city and to verify this age-long item of Biblical history.

And there is being unveiled in the records of ancient Egypt actual knowledge from far beyond the Flood. Those records carry back a long way towards the very gates of the Garden eastward in Eden. They verify the story of the Bible at every point.

Open to attack, subject to testing from every quarter, the Bible stands the test. And the test simply dwarfs the scholarship of modern times.

But the Bible must be contained in small compass. Libraries of literature would be confusing and unusable. Think of the treasures of the library of the British Museum and of the Bodleian library; and then of all the other great libraries of the earth. What a great asset to the nation and nations which possess them. What an asset to civilisation.

And yet who knows anything of these libraries? They are so unwieldy, so complex that they must be housed each in a special building and only specially authorised readers may have access thereto.

The average men, those who pass and re-pass the buildings, thrill with pride at the thought of the wonderful treasures therein contained but know nothing practical of them, and seldom enter them.

Now the Bible covers all the ground that all these libraries cover, but to be so bulky and so exhaustive would be to destroy the practical value of the Bible. So here we have it in one small compact volume which thousands carry around with them at their daily tasks, and many copies occupy a place on the various tables of the home.

Human ability has never succeeded in so condensing knowledge elsewhere as in the Bible. Why, if men have failed to so condense everywhere else, should men succeed in accomplishing the task to perfection in the Bible?

IF THESE MEN OF GOD WERE NOT INSPIRED THEN THEY SHOWED POWERS OF MIND AND A RANGE OF KNOWLEDGE INFINITELY SUPERIOR TO THE BEST SCHOLARSHIP OF TO-DAY.

IT IS THE GLORY OF THE MOST PRETENTIOUS SCHOOLS OF TO-DAY THAT THEY ARE ABLE TO CRITICISE (mark the word) TO CRITICISE THE BIBLE. WHO AMONG THEM WOULD UNDERTAKE WITH ALL THE KNOWLEDGE OF THIS SELF-SATISFIED AGE TO PRODUCE SUCH A BIBLE?

One is reminded of the description of such schools in the book of *Revelation*:

"Thou sayest I am rich and increased with goods and have need of nothing; and knowest not that thou art wretched and miserable and poor and blind and naked. I counsel thee to buy of me gold tried in the fire, that thou mayest be rich: and white raiment that thou mayest be clothed, and that the shame of thy nakedness do not appear; and anoint thine eyes with eye-salve that thou mayest see. As many as I love I rebuke and chasten. Be zealous therefore and repent.
"Behold I stand at the door and knock: if any man hear My voice, and open the door, I will come in to him, and sup with him and he with Me.
"To him that overcometh will I grant to sit with Me in My throne even as I also overcame, and am sat down with my Father in His throne.

"He that hath an ear let him hear what the spirit saith unto the churches."

What a triumph in scholarship, to sit down with Christ the great Teacher in His throne.

That triumph will not come by criticism of the word, but in mastery of the word.

Condensed, portable, usable; all these things we should expect of a Divine revelation. The Bible is all this, and to a degree which has never been approached by any other literature, nor by any school.

The Bible must be filled with the Personality of God, if it be indeed inspired of God.

Every author writes himself into the pages of his book. The reader of Charles Kingsley knows Charles Kingsley better than his next door neighbour knows him that neighbour not being a reader of Charles Kingsley. The reader of Shakespeare knows Shakespeare; while the whole world is left to wonder who Shakespeare the man was, outside of his books.

This is a truism so universal that it is not necessary to labour the statement. If God be the author of the Bible, then the personality of God must be written into the Bible.

Surely this is the case. The God-consciousness leaps out of the pages of the Bible and seizes upon the mind and heart of the reader. From the highest and widest manifestation of God in the Elohim of universal creation, to Jehovah, the God and King of Israel and to Jesus the Redeemer of Israel, the Saviour of men and the ultimate

King of Israel who shall sit upon the throne of His Father David and rule over the House of Jacob for ever, the God-consciousness and the Revelation of God becomes more and more intimate and clear.

With that consciousness the "Word of God is quick and powerful, sharper than a two-edged sword, piercing to the dividing of the soul and spirit and of the joints and marrow, discerning even the thoughts and intents of the heart."

From the first pregnant words, "In the beginning God created the heaven and the earth," down to the last testimony, "Behold I come quickly," God is in the Word and the Word is replete with the living personality of God.

Assuming the Bible to be the revelation of God, then we should expect results from the reading and study of the Word such as can be found in connection with the reading of no other literature.

And such is the case. The regeneration experience which has worked its transforming influence throughout all the generations of God's people, testimonies to which are to be found in all the Bible literature and in all the literature of the Christian church, an unconscious presentation of which fills all history and biography, and this is the positive experience of millions at the present time, although it is to be feared that under Bible criticism, which has so largely replaced Bible study and Bible reading, this experience is less common than it formerly was.

The Bible stands alone in its effect upon the personal experience of the reverent student; and upon the character of nations and races. If the Bible be in very deed the revelation of

God, then we should expect the Bible to bring men into actual relationship with God. And again such is the case. For

"To as many as received Him; to them gave He power to become the sons of God, even as many as believe on His name, which were born, not of blood nor of the flesh, nor of the will of man, but of God." "How then shall they believe on Him of whom they have not heard and how shall they hear without a preacher ..."

and, we may add, how shall they preach unless they have the written word?

Therefore we join with the Apostle John in his exclamation, "Behold what manner of love the Father hath bestowed upon us that we should be called the sons of God."

The Bible fills all the requirements of what is expected of a book given by Divine revelation.

THE ELIMINATIONS FROM THE BIBLE

In order that the Bible may be compact, readable and usable as we find it to-day, instead of being in the form of whole libraries of literature as we find all purely human literature which attempts such a broad field as the Bible undertakes, systematic eliminations have taken place at every stage of the book.

In dealing with astronomical creation and with cosmogony, as we find these mighty fields of enquiry dealt with in the Bible, each branch of science is accorded ONE SENTENCE.

"In the beginning God created the heaven and the earth." Thus is the origin of matter, the origin of the material universe, etc., dealt with in exactly ten words. Why should there be any more? The whole of the related matters are discussed and revealed by that one telegram from heaven. Volumes such as men have written, and would write about the related matters, cannot add one single ray of light, or item of additional information.

"And the earth became empty and desolate." Thus seems to be told the fact of a former creative era having come to its close.

"And darkness was upon the face of the deep." Thus is recorded the cessation of those activities which had previously filled the abounding world with light.

"And the Spirit of God moved upon the face of the waters." Thus we see the Divine activity directed towards a reconstruction of the formless, empty, dark world.

"And God said, Let there be light."

Thus is recorded the starting the machinery of light, giving activity in the world which is about to be made new. A dark solar system has suddenly broken out into light, and now shines as a star of the first magnitude in the heavens.

Thus step by step is the mighty story told in pregnant sentences. How luminous they are and how natural. Universalities are being unrolled before the gaze of men, and as is the use of nature, no one seems to be surprised at the superlative use of words and of ideas.

Train a person's mind to understand words and sentences, but keep from him knowledge of the universe. Let him now approach and read the first chapter of *Genesis*.

Let us suppose such a person came to the passage before us without a concept in his mind as to the origin of things. Understanding what he reads, he will go away with a complete outline of the origin of the universe, of the solar system, of the earth in particular, of life upon it as it appeared stage after stage; and finally of the appearance of man and the beginning of the human era.

Then comes the Sabbath of rest from creative activity.

Now comes another and evidently later chapter in the creation story.

This time the narrative is confined to the earth and to man upon it, with the lower forms of life which were associated with him. It takes up the story where the former chapter ended.

The formation of Adam, the dust of the earth!

What a wonderful statement of the physiology of man. The elements of which he is composed are taken from the earth. Every particle of that which entered into the formation of his physical being is from earth, water and air. The earth supplied the original materials; the earth sustains them to the end of individual life and to the last of the generations of mankind. Well for the man that this is the case. It would be awkward to require materials for the upkeep of the body which the earth failed to supply. There are no means of transport of such materials from other spheres. What a wealth of meaning is in the short sentence, "And the Lord God formed man of the dust of the earth." The chemist can, with labour, analyse the body to-day and find that this is exactly the case. He will find familiar chemicals entering into the make-up of the human body, and of foreign material not a particle. But this is all said in ten short words.

The Divine breathing into the senseless chemical compound which has been formed into the body of the man is thus stated. "And God breathed into his nostrils the breath of life, and man became a living soul." That sentient man should be made to arise from the dust of the earth, – and no scientist can deny that he does so arise, – and that he returns to his native dust again, is a greater miracle daily taking place before our eyes than was the resurrection of Lazarus. It is a greater miracle than will be the resurrection from the dead. It is easier to restore than to create. Let those who talk about miracles as something foreign to nature lay their hands upon their mouths before this perennial miracle, and be still.

Every babe that is born, every generation that succeeds the

other, is a constant continuance of the miracle which, as far as the Adamic race is concerned, began with the formation of man and the inbreathing of the breath of life into Adam, the father of us all.

It is all told in about thirty words.

The garden, and the placing of the man – twenty words.

The botany of the garden – forty-three words.

The geography of the garden – one hundred and four words.

The appointment of the man to the care of the garden – twenty-two words.

The promulgation of Divine law, "And the Lord God commanded the man." This is the fountain head of Divine jurisprudence. In all the law literatures of the world there is not a more pregnant sentence than this. It is the establishment of the Divine will as the energising and guiding power which should henceforth control the life of the man.

Herein is the man different from the beast. The beast does his own instinctive will. Unregenerate man does his own will as far as his fellow men will allow him to do so. But the man, who is regenerate, as was the man Adam before the fall, does the will of God.

This is the heart of the commandments later revealed in code form to Moses. This is the law as ratified by Jesus Christ in the Sermon on the Mount. This is the meaning of the prayer taught us by Our Lord, "Thy kingdom come. Thy will be done on earth as it is in heaven."

The ability to comprehend and do the will of God marks the man created in the likeness of God.

"And the Lord God commanded the man" - forty-seven words.

The formation of Adamic language, *Genesis* 2:20-21 – seventy-seven words.

The establishment of the family life of the Adamic race - one hundred and thirteen words.

The dawn of moral consciousness through the stress of temptation. The falling under the stress of temptation.

The judgment of tempter and tempted.

The promise of redemption.

The sentence.

The expulsion from the garden, and the gift of death as a temporary measure of mercy. All this is contained in one short chapter, *Genesis* 3.

These short sentences tell the whole history of a phase of human existence. How long no man may say. The life of man prior to the fall was deathless and therefore probably did not number days nor years. But from the moment the sentence of death was pronounced upon Adam, time was the measurer of his life and so was counted carefully to the end. What brevity! What fulness! What clarity! This is the finger of God.

Chapter four gives us the most tragic chapter of world history subsequent to the fall of man. It is the story of the birth of the first born sons of the Adamic race; the institution of sacrificial worship foreshadowing the promised atonement for sin; the schism of Cain, who offered bloodless sacrifices; the murder of Abel the protomartyr; the judgment of Cain; the final defection of Cain expressed in the following pregnant words, "CAIN WENT OUT FROM THE PRESENCE OF JEHOVAH."

It follows the generations of Cain far enough to show that

Lamech boasted of murder, "I have slain a man to my wounding, and a young man to my hurt."

And the proclamation of revenge as a principle of action, "If Cain shall be avenged seven fold, truly Lamech seventy and seven fold."

This is the end of that tragic chapter, as far as it is written in the Bible.

Here begins one of the great eliminations from the Bible. Never again is the name Jehovah mentioned in relation to Cain; and except as they impinge upon the appointed seed, the Cain descent has henceforth no place in the Bible story. They have no part in working out the redemption and the atonement; therefore they are not carried forward in the histories of the Bible.

Just twenty-four short verses of chapter four to tell the whole of this tragic story.

And now begins a new line of descent and a new story of the descent of man from God.

How simple is the story. The last two verses of chapter four introduce the theme. The theme is the creation of Adam and Eve in the likeness of God, and the birth to them of a son after their likeness, whose name is called Seth; that is to say, the appointed seed.

BUT WHERE ARE CAIN AND HIS DESCENDANTS?

"Cain went out from the presence of the Lord" and neither he nor his seed are in the "appointed" line.

What a wonderful book would have been written of the development of Cain and his seed under the guiding hand of Jehovah, had Cain by repentance and faith returned to his God. But Cain went out, as far as this book is concerned - for ever.

So we have the new beginning of the appointed seed. What a thin red line it is. God; Adam, Seth – Noah, Shem – Abraham, Isaac, Jacob, Israel.

Think of the teeming world filled with interesting things of which the author of the Bible might have caused a record to be preserved. Think of the few sentences pregnant with meaning, in which the religious, moral and racial facts of the early ages of the race are recorded. Only a few words, yet causing to stand out with terrible clearness the spiritual declension of the race and the resultant tragedy of the flood. How clear it is made that the whole world had corrupted itself. This is too frequently considered to be in the matter of morality and spirituality only. But should not the physical be also understood? Was not the earth the victim of all that deadly brood of diseases which flow from a venereal beginning? Is it not to be understood that the race of men was dying by its own corruption and suffering horribly in the process? Must we not assume that the flood was in the nature of a drastic remedy to cut short agony rather than a drastic punishment for rebellion? Must we not see in it both justice and mercy?

The elimination of Japhet and Ham; the descendants of Ishmael; and of Esau from the continued record stands out clearly. Further, the elimination from the record of all those sections of the Israel people who did not, during the ages of the national residence of Israel in Palestine, dwell within the geographical boundaries of the land.

For instance, that part of the tribe of Judah which descended from Zarah, which left the Israel organisation, was excluded from the narrative of the Bible. They were included in the covenants, but excluded from the histories.

Again, the tribe of Dan marched out beyond the boundary of the land. From the time they did so they marched out from the histories of the people. They were still in the covenant, but were excluded from the histories of the Bible.

Only that official organisation which has through the ages represented Israel is included within the scope of the narrative of the Bible.

Events occurring within the national life of Israel, but which had no bearing upon the onward march of the Divine purpose in Israel were excluded. "Are they not written in the book of – ." This is a formula often used. But the great majority of things have no mention at all in the sacred volume.

Explanations of things which are fully given in the later Scriptures are excluded from the earlier Scriptures. Explanations which are fully given in the early Scriptures are not repeated in the later Scriptures. Thus all repetition of doctrine and explanation is avoided in this most wonderful book.

For instance Our Saviour preached during all His ministry the gospel of the Kingdom. This we find asserted, illustrated and preached in the Gospels. But we do not find an explanation of what the Gospel of the Kingdom is in the New Testament. Why? Because it is fully explained in the Old Testament. The 19th and 20th chapters of *Exodus* give the most graphic account of that. It is the bringing of the nation, Jehovah the God and King of the nation, and the law together, the three essential elements of the Kingdom.

This is the Kingdom which Jesus preached, God's will being the law of the nation administered by Himself, and honoured and kept in the nation. This is the Gospel of the Kingdom which Jesus preached, and this is the Kingdom which He will finally administer as King.

The result of the elimination of all matters not bearing on the national and individual messages of the Gospel secures for us a Bible literature which is compact and usable for the scholar and for the man in the street.

Every historical reference must be right. Every scientific adjustment must be true. Every doctrinal teaching must be righteous. But not a single such reference, statement, or doctrine must be looked for which is not essential to the grand plan of the revealed word.

A universal literature which can be carried in the pocket of the business man is the triumph of the Divinely inspired book.

RESTATEMENTS OF THE BIBLE

We are now to consider a most important feature of the activities (we use the word advisedly) of the Scriptures of truth.

To think of the Bible as one Book cast into one form which was constructed little by little through some twelve hundred years, finally attaining completion with the addition of the book of *Revelation*, is, we submit, to misunderstand the history of the sacred Scriptures. There is good literary reason for believing that every age had a full statement of the facts of creation; the prospective development of the Adamic family; the establishment in due time of the Israel people; the coming of the Redeemer; the progress and mission of Israel in the latter days; and the final millennial consummation at the end of the age.

The *Egyptian Book of the Dead* seems to know this to have been the case in the earliest days. The *Genesis* narrative, the *Book of Jasher*, etc., show preachers of righteousness – notably Enoch and Noah – prior to the flood; Melchizedek, Priest of the Most High God, was such a majestic personage that it is written of him that Jesus Christ "was made a Priest for ever after the order of Melchizedek." He brought forth in his priestly ministry bread and wine, and blessed Abraham, using the elements foreshadowing the broken body and shed blood of Our Lord as in our day we make remembrance of the same.

Abraham believed God in connection with the Gospel he foresaw even to "the day" of Our Lord, a point in history not even yet attained.

Abraham, according to Divine testimony, kept the commandments, statutes and laws of Jehovah, the knowledge of which it is clear antedated Sinai and the wilderness teaching.

We are justified in assuming that the revelation thus possessed in the various ages we have named was written and full.

It is quite manifest that the revelation possessed in these early ages was so stated as to be unsuited for later ages; the fundamental truth was the same, but the conditions, both of the truth and of the age to which it must be applied, so differed from later ages as to require local and temporary application of the truth. For instance, everything from the twelfth chapter of *Genesis*, which relates the call of Abram, on to the end of the book of *Revelation* was presented in the form of prophecy, the fulfilment of which had not yet commenced.

It was essential that all that related to those early ages with the emphasis arranged to suit those early conditions should be left behind.

It was even more essential that the foundation things, which must remain the same for all ages until the consummation, should be brought forward. So we have the Creation record; the genealogical descent of the appointed line (Seth) who were the bearers of the covenant of redemption by the seed of the woman. We have also the record of the Flood; the establishment of the Noahic seed in postdiluvian times; we have the separation of the three families; the selection of the Shem descent to be the bearers of the covenant, and the genealogical descent to Abraham. All these things were vital, and are vital still, but because the age had passed to which the emphasis of the early statement of revelation was adjusted, it was necessary that such statement should be left behind.

A new revelation of old truth began again with Abraham, doubtless including the things that we have mentioned as brought forward. It is also manifest that that statement carried a prevision of all that should follow even to the millennial reign of Our Lord. But the emphasis of the statement was adjusted to that age and to the fulfilled conditions of God's plan of truth and action at that stage of world progress.

The emphasis was laid upon the covenants made with Abraham and Sarah, confirmed to Isaac and to Jacob.

Of Abraham, Jesus declared "your father Abraham rejoiced to see my day: and he saw it, and was glad;" whereas the patriarch Jacob-Israel declared "my blessing hath prevailed above that of my progenitors even unto the utmost bound of the everlasting hills."

In connection with the Abrahamic-Israel statement of truth, the emphasis was laid to suit the patriarchal dispensation. Much knowledge of the past, exhaustive knowledge of the then present, and the whole of the future in prophetic prevision were known to the patriarchs and their associates.

Again we say it was essential that all the former mentioned essential things should be brought forward with the essential things of the patriarchal period, and that it was equally essential that the statement, the emphasis of which was adjusted to suit that age, should be left behind.

It is manifest that again a new statement of old truth began at the burning bush where Jehovah gave to Moses, in trust for Israel, a revelation of Himself.

Now "Moses was learned in all the wisdom of the Egyptians," but the wisdom of the Egyptians included all the wonders of Divine revelation which were built into the Great Pyramid, and which were recorded in the *Egyptian Book of the Dead* and other such literature. Moses was therefore not ignorant of the great body of revealed truth, and to his knowledge Jehovah appealed as to the Hebrew revelation which preceded him, saying, "I am the God of your fathers Abraham, Isaac and Jacob."

Laying as a foundation all the essential things which had been brought forward to the end of the patriarchal dispensation, there was added to it all that Divine body of revelation contained in the Mosaic writings from the burning bush forward.

These writings, condensed in form, with every nonessential eliminated, became numbered among the essentials which must henceforth be carried forward from age to age and dispensation to dispensation to the end of time.

But outside of the Mosaic writings contained in the Bible they had other books dealing with the then existing conditions, the emphases of which were suited to that particular time. For instance, they had "the book of the wars of Jehovah" and doubtless many other such works which the same rule required should be left behind with the passing of the conditions and the age.

At least a new emphasis was laid upon old truth, and additional revelation was given at the period of the golden age of Israel in Palestine under David and Solomon. The Bible was enriched by the

Psalms of David and his contemporaries and by the wisdom of Solomon. The statement of truth had its emphasis adjusted to suit the new position of Israel among the nations, and the newly instituted temple worship.

Doubtless there was abundant literature making application of the truth to the age and conditions then obtaining. For instance, we know that Solomon wrote upon a multitude of subjects and of objects, but the writings have been left behind.

There came the time of the division of the kingdoms, Israel from Judah, and the entirely new conditions in Israel and Judah, and also entirely new world conditions with the establishment of the Assyrian and Babylonian Empires.

The emphasis and application of the truth to the age and conditions of David and Solomon would manifestly be out of joint with the conditions that arose upon the division of Israel into two nations.

There was therefore a new statement and a new application of old truth by the prophets, major and minor, to suit the new age and the new conditions. The essential things were brought forward, including the Mosaic books and the Psalms of David, but the statement and emphasis were made to suit the age and conditions then arising, and the local and temporary things concerning the Davidic period were left behind.

There came the time when the House of Israel, the House of Judah, and the House of David had disappeared from Palestine, and from among the captivity of Judah there had returned a handful, in numbers not sufficient to fill the seats at the stadium at Wembley Exhibition, who proceeded to establish themselves in the land as the nation of the Jews.

Again it was necessary that there should be a restatement of truth, and accordingly Ezra and Nehemiah, Zechariah and Malachi added their writings to the preceding sacred Scriptures.

The stream of Israel history in Palestine was falling to a low ebb; it had during the seventy years captivity of Judah dried up altogether.

On the return of the immigrant band, which founded the nation of the Jews, the current of Biblical history began to run again in a narrow stream to find its sudden and complete end with the destruction of Jerusalem and the scattering of the nation of the Jews.

But while the stream of history failed, the glorious outburst of prophecy compensated manifold.

Local and temporary conditions of the time of the existence of the two kingdoms, Israel and Judah, largely passed away, only the essential things being brought forward in the final form of the Old Testament Scriptures.

Finally there came the time of the first advent of Our Lord. Israel conditions and world conditions were such as to call for a new statement of old truth.

Still the essential things must be brought forward; these were condensed into the canon of the Old Testament Scriptures, and now there came the addition of the New. The Gospels recorded the triumphant fulfilment of Messianic prophecy. The Acts of the Apostles recorded the establishment of the Christian dispensation by the outpouring of the Holy Ghost.

The Epistles readjusted the emphasis of the new statement of divine truth to the Christian dispensation, and the book of Revelation carried forward the details of the great seven times of prophecy to the millennial glory, and the issuing in of the eternal condition beyond the close of the seven thousand years of the Adamic period of earth's history.

Thus the emphasis was adjusted to meet the conditions of the Christian dispensation.

But again the emphasis, adjusted two thousand years ago, is beginning to lose touch with the present age.

The gospel of salvation by the grace of God has stood unchanged through every age, and still so stands; perfect in adjustment, complete in statement, the gospel of Christ which is the power of God unto salvation to everyone that believeth. The gospel of the grace of God is not a progressive gospel.

But the gospel of the kingdom, while in the essentials it is the same from age to age, changes in emphasis with the progress of the kingdom, and of the age. Today it is necessary to add to the statement as made down to the closing of the canon of the Scriptures, the fact, the glorious fact, of prophecy fulfilled in Israel, in Judah, in the House of David, in the Babylonian succession of Empires, in the rise of the Moslem and Pontifical powers, and in the miraculous latter day development of Israel-Britain.

That statement will doubtless be made and promulgated with authority upon the coming of Our Lord.

The truth lives on from age to age and God's kingdom nation on earth is working out its fulfilment to the final consummation when Our Lord shall come and reign.

THE BIBLE UNDER ATTACK

T he question is being asked today, Can we trust our Bible? It is right that we should first consider *who it is that raises this question.*

Primarily the question was raised in German Universities. The people who raised the question in German Universities were not the followers of Luther. Let this be taken into consideration most carefully. The supporters of the Reformation never raised the question as to the trustworthiness of the Bible.

Let it be remembered that the Reformation was bitterly opposed by political action; by administrative power, exercised without mercy; and by all the power of the ecclesiastical machine, backed by the power of the Papal States of Europe. Witness the Inquisition. It was made a matter of life and death to possess a copy of the Scriptures and to confess the faith of the Reformation. Even in England, usually so free, men and women went to the stake and were burned by English men and women for the profession of their faith.

They went to their death as martyrs to the truth, innocently condemned. *By their condemnation and execution kings and parliaments, priests and laymen, became guilty of murder in the highest degree, for which they will yet stand at the bar of justice of the King of Israel, and will yet give an accounting for these things, although they have passed away with their own age.*

The physical weapon is not used now in Europe and Britain. *But the struggle against the principles of the Reformation is not yet over.*

The source of the strength of the Reformation was the Bible, the inspired Word of God. This has been true all through the ages. The strength of the resistance to the Reformation was thrown against the Scriptures. It was thrown against the translation of the Scriptures into English. It was thrown against the printing of the Scriptures. It was thrown against the circulation and possession of the Scriptures. But all along the line the fight against the dissemination of the Scriptures was lost.

The weight of the opposition is now thrown against THE INSPIRATION, THE HISTORICITY, AND THE RELIABILITY GENERALLY OF THE SCRIPTURES.

It is a continuation of the fight against the free doctrines of the Reformation.

The attack this time is in the mental world.

It has so far succeeded that many of those who would gladly support the Scriptures have been captured in the mental world and have been made the bondservant of the enemy. They are like Samson Agonistes, captive, with eyes put out, grinding the mills of the Philistines, and making sport for them at the same time. Thus we could name men who believe themselves to be Protestant, and who are active against the claims of those who attack the Reformation in the matter of forms of worship, taking the field with courage and vigour against the Romanizing section of the Church; who are nevertheless actively pushing the propaganda against the historicity and reliability of the Scriptures. These may be sure that the Romanizing element will forgive them all their opposition to Roman ritual as long as they do the work of the Roman Hierarchy in attacking the inspiration and historicity of the Scriptures.

The Modernist attack upon the reliability and the inspiration of the Scriptures *is being engineered by those who have never ceased to attack the Reformation, and the open Bible.*

But these are not working alone.

Take the list of the outstanding fathers of the Modernist attack upon the Bible, whose names have been the leading names with which to conjure in the German Universities, from Wellhausen upwards, and it will be found that they are German Jews.

The Jew is in the closest sympathy with everything which will tend to overthrow not the Reformation only, but also the whole of the Christian faith. Thus they have joined with all their mental power in the attack upon the Bible.

These two forces, Jesuit and Jew, have combined to attack the foundations of our faith, namely, the Bible. They have secured the co-operation of Protestant British men, of England, Scotland and America, and together the attack has been made.

The *supporters of the Reformation* have been caught asleep. Their attacking power never existed during these last generations. They slept on the laurels their fathers had won with the expense of life and fortune. They shepherded in a perfunctory manner the descendants of the sheep their fathers had gathered, scattering to them with none too liberal hand the supplies of Biblical food their fathers had prepared. So peaceful was the time that they neither prepared to defend their charge, nor to attack the enemies of the faith.

Thus the last generation of the supporters of the Reformation were routed, horse, foot and artillery. Those who maintained their ground did so more because their particular charges had not been acutely subjected to the attacks of the modernist enemy.

But now the enemy is within their walls at every point and is attacking the validity of the Bible. Thus we say that the question as to the validity of the Scriptures was raised by the Jesuit and the Jew. They have made it appear by partial statements of fact and wrong statements that there is not reliability such as our fathers believed in, in the sacred Scriptures. The time has come for the forces which defend the Reformation to rally. And the first step we have indicated is to reconnoitre the enemy. The next step is to consider, *who, within the ranks of the church and nation of the Reformation, are working in harmony with the enemy.*

The Jesuit is still pressing his campaign to overthrow the Protestant faith. His own writings up to date will give absolute proof of that.

The Jew is still pressing his campaign, and is doing so hand in hand with the Jesuit. His own writings will also make this clear.

The modernist within our ranks, and especially within the Universities, is acting with both of these, although unconsciously.

All of these are calling into question the reliability of the Scriptures.

Such then are the forces which are attacking the Scriptures.

The next thing necessary to do is to *reconnoitre their methods.*

METHODS OF ATTACK

The chief attention has been focused on the Scriptures. Regarding these they have assumed certain definite positions.

They have represented that there is confusion arising from the various names of God in the Bible. Each name is supposed to have represented, in the beginning, a different religion. From the sources of such religions it has been assumed the original Bible materials were drawn. These materials were then supposed to have been worked in together to form the text of the Holy Scriptures, the various names of God being retained in the documents so incorporated. Thus Wellhausen and all his followers.

From this citadel these must now withdraw. It is an untenable position.

They have represented that there is more than one story of the creation, and that these do not agree with each other. It was a fatal move for the wing of the enemy of the Bible when he entered into this citadel. *There are not two or more accounts of the creation.* There is one sequent account dealing with progressive stages of creation history. From this position modern scholarship will have to withdraw.

They have caused it to be believed that science has demonstrated the theory of evolution against the Biblical account of the creation. As a matter of fact this is not true. Science has demonstrated no such thing.

That there was a progressive creation the Scriptures assert and the defenders of the faith of the Reformation believe. But that there has been a continuous evolution and that species ascended from lower forms of life by inherent powers science does not demonstrate, and theologians do not believe. It remains for the philosopher who has an animus against the Bible alone to maintain this statement, which is nowhere shown to be the fact. Those who assert and maintain this to be the case are the left wing of the forces attacking the Scriptures. Many will say, Why should we trouble about that? God either worked by successive creative acts, or once for all He placed within the orders of life the inherent power to ascend in the scale of being.

If we were simply seeking for an explanation of God and of His methods of working in His universe, it might not be a matter of great importance. If we were Mohammedans or Buddhists making the same enquiry, even if we were Roman Catholics who build their faith on, and accept as the final authority, the voice of the church, it might not be for us a matter of prime importance. But being *Christians who build upon the written Word of God,* it is of the first importance to us.

It is because it is so important to the Protestant Christian that the integrity of the Word should be maintained, that the creation narrative is thus being so persistently attacked. If faith in the Word can be shaken in the mind of the Christian *then he will easily turn to the voice of the Church,* or at all events *he will turn away from his living Christian faith.* The first would satisfy the Jesuit, the second, the Jew.

Therefore the creation narrative has been attacked and the evolutionary theory has been substituted. For if the latter be true, the Bible is held to be mistaken and therefore not inspired.

Therefore it is said that science has established the theory of evolution. Science has done no such thing.

So patently is this the case that evolutionists have in part ceased to state that it is so, but are saying, "It is generally accepted by the best scholars." But the best scholars to speak for science are scientists. The leading men in that realm are declaring that evolution has not been demonstrated, but remains only a working hypothesis. For instance, Sir Oliver Lodge says, the term evolution means only a process of creation. But a process of creation is that which the Bible sets forth. The whole evolution movement will have failed of its aim if this be the accepted definition. Then, instead of disturbing faith in the Scriptures it will confirm it.

From the statement that science has demonstrated evolution the attacking forces must now withdraw.

So far good.

BIBLICAL FACTORS

Doubtless much useful work has been done by textual and even by higher criticism. When an army enters a field and undertakes military works, the works so constructed are usable by either side, as one or other of the armies possesses the field.

Thus in the First World War the Germans prepared the material for the building of the pipe line to Jerusalem, which should carry water to the army marching across the desert. That preparation fell into the hands of the British and was used by them to defeat the enemy, and to water the land.

The higher critics have done much that will be usable to the rising generation of the defenders of the Reformation, who will shortly enter into their labours.

What are the documents upon which the higher critics have expended so much time and labour?

There is not one original document remaining of all the books and letters of the Old Testament and the New.

The critic has therefore been expending his time upon transcriptions, transliterations, and translations of the original documents.

As we have seen, the restatements of the Bible have been constant from age to age and from dispensation to dispensation.

The original documents of any one statement have not been permitted to be brought forward. Knowing our tendency to idolatry, the reason for this is very clear.

If we were left to depend on the text of the documents alone we should be unable to fully examine their origins so as to reach by that measure alone assurance of their inspiration. Thus the scholar who confines himself to the text of the Bible finds himself in difficulty.

Thus far the critic has been able to go. He has been able and in fact been forced by the evidence in his hands to the conclusion that many things in the Bible are ancient, and have been brought forward from the earliest times.

Thus it is with the creation records; and with the record of the flood; and the history of Abraham; and as to the organisation of Israel the nation; and as to the throne of David; and as to the separation of the two kingdoms; and as to the captivities; and as to the establishment of the nation of the Jews; and as to the New Testament Scriptures.

Thus it is as to the laws of Israel (national law); and as to the ordinances of Israel (ecclesiastical law); and as to the covenants made with the fathers; and as to the covenant made with the nation Israel; thus it is with the covenant made with the House of David, and as to the New Covenant, made and promulgated through Jeremiah, and, etc., etc.

All these and other things are so constantly brought forward that they cannot be doubted or gainsaid.

But God has not left us with the written text of the Scriptures alone upon which to build.

He has given to us *the contents of the Scriptures.* That is to say, the lands, the things, the peoples and the nations of which the Scriptures speak. With the contents of the Scriptures the higher critic has not very largely concerned himself. Perhaps the reason is that had he done so he would have demonstrated the inspiration of the Scriptures. That neither Jesuit nor Jew desired to do, before the eyes of Protestant Christianity.

We, however, will turn our attention to the contents of the Scriptures. Let us summarise.

Concerning the human race the Scriptures begin and proceed as follows:—

The creation of man.

The formation of Adam.

The birth of Cain and Abel.

The death of Abel.

The defection of Cain.

The birth of Seth, the father of the "appointed" seed.

The descent from Seth to Noah and the tremendous events of the time.

The selection of Shem to be the covenant bearer.

The descent from Shem to Abraham.

The call of Abraham.

The Abrahamic covenant.

Isaac.

Jacob.

The establishment of Israel.

The setting up of the national administration, lay and clerical.

Israel's induction into the Promised Land.

The establishment of the throne.

The division of the Kingdoms.

The captivities.

The setting up of the Jewish nation.

The first coming of Our Lord.

The establishment of the Kingdoms of Babylon and of Britain (Israel in the Isles), *Daniel* 2.

The Babylonian succession of Empires (Imperial and Ecclesiastical).

Israel-Britain's continuance through the seven times of prophecy.

The fall of the Babylon Empires.

The miraculous expansion of Britain to a universal kingdom.

The coming of our Lord to reign.

This is an outline of the scope of the contents of the Bible. The plan has been unfalteringly proclaimed from the earliest ages. The people have marched alongside the Bible, with unfaltering tread, throughout the ages.

Again we must associate *the people of the Bible* with the book itself: The Bible has always been incarnate in the people.

No human pre-vision could have pre-written the history of the people, in outline and detail, as that history is pre-written in the Bible.

The continuous life and development of the people, the whole history of which is in the Bible from the beginning to the end, is God's demonstration of the reliability and inspiration of the Bible.

The text of the Scriptures may not satisfy the mind, for God did not rest the proof of inspiration there alone, but when the contents of the Bible, fulfilled in the life of the people, are added to the text, these demonstrate Divine inspiration.

From Seth the son of Adam, "who was the Son of God," to the present generation, there has never been a break in the continuous descent, nor in the prophecy-fulfilling progress of the people of the Bible.

Thus we say that together with the documents of the Bible, and the contents of the Bible, must be studied exhaustively the history of the people of the Bible. That is to say, the history of the "appointed seed."

These latter we have not the slightest room to doubt are Israel. We must uncover and study the history of these.

Israel in Bible history is to be found in two main stages.

(1) United Israel, including all the twelve tribes.

(2) Israel of the ten tribes separated from Judah and Benjamin. *These disappear from Bible history* when they were carried into captivity by Assyria.

The prophecies then take up the theme and present to us *Israel in the Isles.* To these come in due time the Israel of the captivity,

As we read *the prophecies* of the Bible, and *the histories* which throw light on Israel in captivity, we are assured that Britain is none other than the Israel "in the Isles" of the Bible.

Prior to the days of the captivities of Israel and Judah this British colony existed as a Brith (covenant) colony, but it was without the throne of David. The foundation of the colony was the Zarah-Judah migration from Troy before the time of David.

To this colony in due time the throne of David came, and the colony then became the kingdom which "the God of Heaven" set up (*Daniel* 2).

Nearly a millennium later, the descendants of the ten-tribed captivity came and established themselves in these islands, forcibly joining the Kingdom.

All this fulfils to the very letter the prophetic prewriting of the history of the "appointed seed."

The scholar who has not honestly and seriously examined all this really is not in a position to give a conclusion as to critical study of the Bible.

The book and the people live together as one.

ECCLESIASTICAL FULFILMENT.

Once again, having taken into account *the national outline* shown from the beginning in the Scriptures, and fulfilled throughout four thousand years of national history, the scholar must also take into count *the ecclesiastical fulfilment.* The national life and activity of the people, on the material plane, is termed "The House of Jacob." The spiritual life of the people is termed the "Israel" experience.

In regard to the ecclesiastical or spiritual life he must tabulate the Messianic prophecies, and he must see that they were all fulfilled in Christ as far as they refer to His first coming.

He must take into account *the creative change* predicted for those who accept the Word as true and *exercise living faith* in the incarnate Word. He must account for that biological change *which makes of the natural man a new creation.* He must explain how it is that up to the time of regeneration *the man was without spiritual conception and perception; but after that change he is endowed with spiritual conception and perception.*

It is not possible to deny this. The testimony is too sure, and too multiple. That testimony is found in the Scriptures from the beginning.

It is a testimony which is written into the biography and history of the Christian Church throughout all the ages.

It is a testimony given by multitudes individually and collectively today.

No court on earth would rule such testimony out.

No court on earth would come to any other conclusion but that *the new creative experience comes to men through the Word of God alone.*

Here is a psychological phenomenon which is surely attested, and must be explained. It is the pre-designed result of the Word of God operating in the life of the people of God.

Moreover, we have the Word *incarnate in Jesus Christ.*

When we take all these and other factors in hand, we are amazed that any body of sincere scholars should ask the Christian world to take account only of the uncertain efforts of the critical school, which confines itself to the written documents. They have held the attention of the people to a part of the study too long. Let them complete their education or give way to others.

But if they complete their education along the lines indicated, there will be an end of modern criticism and in its place will be a far more satisfactory thing, namely, modern demonstration of the inspiration of the Word of God.

THE BIBLE DIVINELY CONFIRMED

IN the last five chapters we have considered the Bible from the standpoint of its compactness of expression; from the standpoint of its eliminations; from the standpoint of its restatements; and from the standpoint of the factors which make an estimation of it possible.

We now come to the most important question, *How shall we be assured that the statement of truth* in the Bible as we possess it to-day is in very deed the Word of God?

Naturally this must be a question which shall be settled for us by authority.

We cannot accept *the voice of the church;* if for no other reason than that the church has never spoken with a united voice since the days of the Apostles.

We cannot accept the voice of scholarship in the matter, for the scholars have not the original documents in hand, and their investigations are blocked, doubtless by Divine providence.

We cannot accept the voice of man in regard to the matter, for the voice of man is ever pronouncing error from which man has subsequently to withdraw.

This is a matter for the voice of God.

But how shall we hear the voice of God?

Through the lips of Jesus Christ the Son of God.

This is the point at which we must arrive, when we persist in ultimate enquiry as to the Scriptures of Truth.

The records of the words of Our Lord are sufficiently clear, and they are historically established.

The authority of Our Lord is questioned by some schools in this generation. They declare Christ spoke according to the vision of His age: He spoke according to the knowledge of His class. His age was not the best informed and His class was that of the mechanical worker, not of the scholar.

Compared with that, this school goes on to say, the vision of the present age is much broader and much clearer; and the knowledge of the modern schools is much more accurate than was that of the class to which Our Lord belonged, and according to which He spake.

They say He was a good man. He taught a wonderful system of ethics. But HE WAS NOT A SCHOLAR.

Well; one is a little nonplussed at the foolishness and the effrontery of it all. Let us consider.

Christ was a good and a great man!

Christ preached the greatest system of ethics the world has ever received!

The personality of Christ has been the most potent factor for good the world has ever known!

But, say they, CHRIST WAS NOT A SCHOLAR. The voice of the modern scholar is superior in the field of scholarship to His voice.

Now let us look at this for a moment.

Christ preached the gospel of the Kingdom, and the gospel of Atonement. He also preached the gospel of His second coming as king as set forth in the Old Testament. This is historic.

Christ gathered His disciples, and finally commissioned them to go into all the world and preach the gospel to every creature.

The disciples accordingly became His apostles, and carried the gospel to the ends of the earth.

TO ADMINISTER THAT GOSPEL THE HOLY GHOST CAME, AND TO ADMINISTER IT HE HAS REMAINED THROUGHOUT ALL THE CHRISTIAN DISPENSATION.

By the preaching of that gospel the regenerating experience has come to countless numbers.

That gospel has been the salt of the earth which has saved the nations from utter decay. According to the simplicity and sincerity in which they have held and lived that gospel the nations have prospered. In departing from it they have perished, such of them as have perished.

The result of that gospel has been *the Christian civilisation,* which means, for the last ages, *world civilisation.*

In holding that gospel in sincerity and obedience civilisation has been exalted. In departing from it civilisation has been degraded. Compared with other faiths, the Christian faith has carried the sincere Protestant Christian nations to a height of purity and power unknown elsewhere in the world.

Now will anyone be foolish enough, having given con-sideration to all this, to proclaim the personality which lies at the base of all this to be that of an ordinary man, an unlettered man, of the peasant class, and with the knowledge only of his class?

Would the Holy Ghost descend from heaven to take up and press the gospel of such a man, or of any man?

Let us not be foolish. The power of that Personality is greater than the power of the greatest of men.

Moreover, the power of the least of men who has with intelligence and reality drunk of the Spirit of Christ, and has been endued with the Holy Spirit, if he lose sight of his own will and of his own opinion, is greater than the greatest of men, equally equipped otherwise, but who has not put on Christ nor drunk of His Spirit.

The power of the nation that is energised by that Personality is greater than that of other nations. This has been made clear through long historic ages.

After nineteen hundred years we are able to estimate the power of the Personality of that obscure Babe which was born in the little city of Bethlehem. And that Personality is greater far than that of an ordinary man, even the best of men.

Moreover, the knowledge of Our Lord rings true at every turn. His age was possessed with many false ideas and ideals. He had none of them. With the things of the past He was acquainted. With the things of His age He showed the utmost familiarity. With the things of the future He showed an equally exact knowledge. In these things He went far beyond the knowledge of the schools, past or present. His knowledge shines forth as simply as the sunlight, and as clearly. You do not as a rule look at the sunlight. You use it as a medium by which to look at other matters. You do not as a rule look at the knowledge of Christ, nor ask from whence it came, although His contemporaries did so ask, but you use the knowledge of the Christ as a medium through which to look at other things. Stop and estimate the quality of the knowledge of the Christ, and one will recognise with reverence that it is Divine.

All other voices, all other authorities, should bow before His voice and before His authority. Should they not do so, it would show exceedingly poor taste and blindness to the obvious glory of the Son of God.

The credentials of Our Lord as the final authority are beyond question.

Now comes the important enquiry: Did Our Lord indicate the form and scope of the Scriptures?

He did.

In His hands were the Scriptures as we have them, as far as the Old Testament is concerned.

Our Lord thus set for the use of the Christian dispensation the authority and form of the Old Testament. He did not form the book. He ratified it.

Now the fact that Our Lord ratified the Old Testament gave to us the Scriptures as He used them, with His own seal and authority, as the canon of the Old Testament for the use of the Christian era.

This is a most important thing.

When the higher critic presses beyond the ratification of Our Lord, and when he makes statements that are not in accord with Our Lord, then he sets his own authority above that of Our Lord.

In order to do this he impugns the scholarship of Our Lord.

The question then comes vividly before us, Whose voice shall we receive as the authoritative voice; the modern scholar's voice, who works at such disadvantage? He is lacking in the very things which Our Lord and His contemporaries possessed in the way of original, and then current, literature. He is lacking in what was then existent oral knowledge of the origin of the books and the personality of the prophets who produced them. Even from the standpoint of equal scholarship, what has of late been attempted, and in part recovered, of that ancient lore was the knowledge of the man on the street, and of *the mechanic in the shop* in Our Lord's day. *For let it be remembered that there were no illiterates in Jewry in Our Lord's day.* Scholarship for scholarship, with the knowledge manifested in His addresses; with the materials at His disposal for accurate knowledge as to the original Scriptures and their history, one would rather accept the knowledge of Christ, being such a man of wisdom and integrity as He is, than we would accept the voice of the modern scholar, handicapped as he is by the lapse of thousands of years, time and the disappearance of all original literature.

But when we recognise the tremendous potentialities which have shown themselves in, and which have flowed through His life, we say that we should be foolish, as is the scholar who enters light-heartedly into the vain competition, if we were to accept the scholar at his own estimate as superior to the Christ in this matter.

We will accept the voice of Our Lord as the final authority. If certain scholars disagree with this, so much the worse for the scholars. Other scholars, equal in all things to such a school, accept with gladness the voice of authority from Our Lord. Such are doubly blessed who can add to their own scholarship the knowledge of Our Lord.

Now for the authoritative utterances of Our Lord.

In the first great act of His public ministry, the preaching the Sermon on the Mount, He set His seal upon the law and the prophets as they were then possessed by the leaders of God's people.

Thus He spake:
"Think not that I am come to destroy the law, or the prophets: I am not come to destroy, but to fulfil. For verily I say unto you, till heaven and earth pass, one jot or one tittle shall in no wise pass from the law, till all be fulfilled."

Throughout all His ministry he preached the gospel of the Kingdom. This He read to them, and expounded to them from the Old Testament Scriptures. What a wonderful satisfaction it is to us of the Christian era to know that Our Lord took the very Scriptures we have so freely in our hands, and made the reading and the expounding of them the daily task of His ministry. We have a beautiful incident recorded which illustrates this.

"And he came to Nazareth, where he had been brought up; and, as his custom was, he went into the synagogue on the sabbath day, and stood up for to read.

"And there was delivered unto him the book of the prophet Esaias. And when he had opened the book, he found the place where it was written.

"The Spirit of the Lord is upon me, because he hath anointed me to preach the gospel to the poor; he hath sent me to heal the broken hearted, to preach deliverance to the captives, and recovering of sight to the blind, to set at liberty them that are bruised,

"To preach the acceptable year of the Lord.

"And he closed the book, and he gave it again to the minister, and sat down. And the eyes of all them that were in the synagogue were fastened on him.

"And he began to say unto them, This day is this scripture fulfilled in your ears.

"And all bare him witness, and wondered at the gracious words which proceeded out of his mouth" *Luke* 4: 16-22.

All through His ministry He used and insisted upon the Scriptures as to every portion, and in fact as to every jot and tittle of them, as the only foundation and as the ultimate authority. Even His own actions were ordered "That it might be fulfilled which was spoken by the prophets." This is the formula of His own life. Should it be less than that for His followers?

After the resurrection, we have that wonderfully beautiful, and infinitely important, report of His conversation with the two disciples as they walked together to Emmaus, and later with all the disciples in the upper room.

"Then said he unto them, O fools, and slow of heart to believe all that the prophets have spoken:
"Ought not Christ to have suffered these things, and to enter into His glory?
"And beginning at Moses and all the prophets, he expounded unto them in all the scriptures the things concerning himself....

"And they said one to another, 'Did not our heart burn within us, while He talked with us by the way, and while He opened to us the scriptures?'

"And He said unto them, These are the words which I spake unto you while I was yet with you, that all things must be fulfilled, which were written in the law of Moses, and in the prophets, and in the psalms, concerning Me.
"Then opened He their understanding, that they might understand the scriptures.
"And said unto them, Thus it is written, and thus it behoved Christ to suffer, and to rise from the dead the third day:
"And that repentance and remission of sins should be preached in His name among all nations, beginning at Jerusalem.
"And ye are witnesses of these things"
Luke 24:25-27; 32; 44-48.

What a wonderful principle is here which must lie at the base of all criticism or estimation of the Scriptures. It is this: –

Our Lord has officially and unmistakably confirmed the Bible statement contained in the Old Testament as we have the same. Beyond His declaration, with which He began, with which He continued, and with which He ended His ministry it is presumption, in the realm of scholarship and in the realm of faith for any of us to go except as a means by which we may add to our knowledge of the truth in harmony with His spoken word.

As to the New Testament. The Holy Spirit has just as surely set His seal to the New Testament, and has backed it for ages by His own power, as did Our Lord to the Old Testament.

We have then the Scriptures, prepared and passed on to the Christian dispensation bearing the seal of Our Lord and of the Holy Ghost. Let the questionings of no man, nor of any school of men, disturb the well grounded faith of the people of God in the Scriptures of Truth.